A TRILLION TINY AWAKENINGS

Candy Royalle was one of Australia's most prominent performing writers. She was a multi-award winning storyteller, activist, educator, singer and vulnerability advocate who shared confronting, political, human and heart-wrenching narratives to audiences all over Australia and the world. She performed at many folk, music, writers and arts festivals globally. Her work and opinion pieces have been featured in *Fairfax*, *The Guardian*, *Overland Literary Journal Online*, *SBS*, *ABC*, *Runway*, *Art Almanac* and many other outlets. She will be remembered by her family and friends as well as the arts, activism and LGBTQIA+ communities for her talent, strength, conviction, passion and firm belief in the power of love to bring about change.

A TRILLION TINY AWAKENINGS

Candy Royalle

UWA PUBLISHING

First published in 2018 and reprinted 2018 by
UWA Publishing
Crawley, Western Australia 6009
www.uwap.uwa.edu.au

UWAP is an imprint of UWA Publishing
a division of The University of Western Australia

ISBN: 9781760800086

A catalogue record for this
book is available from the
National Library of Australia

Cover design by Upside Creative
Typeset in Bembo by Lasertype
Printed by McPherson's Printing Group

This project has been assisted by the Australian Government through
the Australia Council, its arts funding and advisory body.

 uwapublishing

i will dance and resist and dance and persist.
this heartbeat is louder than death...

Suheir Hammad

Mum, I learnt strength and survival from you
Baba, you taught me to question everything
Bro, we have lived the definition of unconditional love
I live for the three of you

Foreword

Ali Cobby Eckermann

// It's a requirement / of the successful artist / to forget what it is / to be humble / so / she's immortal in the mortified kind of way / in the way Eve is / retold over and over / until everyone believes it //

Powerful words from a humble poet: the feminist, queer, daughter of migrants, justice-seeker, the tyrant to the tyrannical, unapologetic, strong in the faith of the oppressed. In this fine collection of poetry, the words of Candy Royalle resound off the page, beyond her living years cut short by a sickness that refused to loosen its grip.

// Come take these stories out of her mouth / relieve her of the swelling / come be a witness / remove the regrets / from that empty loving / she's making progress / moving away from the constant excesses / compassion and forgiveness / she's the other coming / until those colours suffocate / she's walking the streets / near enough to be here / just keep watching her suffer //

These poems are the mark of that ongoing battle. Candy's words are an ocean attempting to smash any walls that confine, the activist and her complete love for woman churning inward and out until in the still of night, there is only an ebb. *A Trillion Tiny Awakenings* contains the tide of her to fill us with the memory of her that cannot recede.

Each one of us has a need to be loved. It is a basic human right refused to many. The verses written here are an ongoing plea for intimacy across the world, an intimacy for the self and the selfless. Candy's words amplify her needs, the desire for love on the front line of a war that has a capacity to harden the softest of hearts, to cut out what was once there, to belittle the beloved.

This isn't another love poem
emptied as I've been by the world's ache
every atlas a tome of violent suffering

Despite her illness Candy remained devout to her passions. Personal love becomes a reflection for her need for a righteous world. Her words throw a challenge to the capacity of the oppressor, to understand the beauty of the other, the beguiling strength of the oppressed. Candy saw the world in all its forms, and through her eyes her wonder of creativity is a gift to us all.

I will leave heavier in the knowledge
that what I sought
and thought I'd found
I have lost again

These words come at a cost to my heart. My friend has died, and I write these words in the absence of her. The love we shared was harnessed by our words, the passion we shared for our views of fairness and for justice to be heard, both loudly on and off the page. Our friendship did not waver from that sharing of respect. And now in her passing it remains so.

Contents

vanquished

your pale skin beneath me
veins feint scrawled blue lines
written in a rush

told you I was colonising you
my form of resistance:
sleeping with white women

you laughed
grinding harder against me
I was

decolonising my tongue
against your cunt
resisting occupation

by pushing inside you
created countries
divided up your body arbitrarily

13 days later
you loved me enough
to invade

crossed continents
occupied my bed
no treaties

just an unravelling
your troops threading
across me

you and clenched fingers
blue grey eyes
dammed water

as you whispered
the sacredness of our
fucking

I gathered your wants
twisted those vines
round an aorta

pumping against your mouth
my hearth thrummed
against your lips

fucking is a violence
we're all versed in
a hammering

you fucked me
in ways I couldn't fuck you
my violence was

fist in mouth
in ears
no

pummelled into
a mess so enormous
you fled

you weren't gone
until 10,000 air miles
were between us

an autonomous withdrawal
me pleading for you
to rebuild your settlements

that was your triumph:
I was Fiji
inviting your invasion

you weren't laughing anymore
skypewhatsappfacetime cold war
we have to speak in skin

I can't reach you
with ones and zeros
spinning grim

come back
you and your
cock and bull troops

come back
these peace talks
are transparent time-killing

you seek another outpost
to plant your flag
I'm a nation

at war with itself
tearing cells from particles
from meat

matter dissolving in nuclear
explosions
this is on you

you pulled out too soon
all you ever cared about
was the incursion

once the capture
was complete
you instigated your retreat

...

4

wondering
legs dangling
into an aching abyss

sickness stretches anxiety
chewing gum on the sole of
my shoe

could plunge
end this unknown
for another

here's the
unfair distribution of suffering
between her collagen lips

his muscle mary pecs
tourists snap at my expanse
this is my horizon

abbreviated in their
digital prevarications
for the processing age

there are pixels
spreading across my abdomen
I've seen them

reflected in friends' sympathy
I am being excavated
again

the last of the old houses in the area
know this ruin
inhale the blue

scramble away from
the edge

...

That house

We loved that house
brick and wood
and huge ocean-facing windows

> we loved its cavernous rooms
> its damp kitchen
> where the salt stuck together in the shakers

Even the outside toilet
didn't really bother us
naked midnight runs to the outhouse

> perched strangely
> just off the back deck
> protected from nosy neighbours

bamboo stretching for stars
sounds of the urban night
punctuated by possums

> … or possibly rats
> bending the long poles, leaping on the next
> and all while we peed

We created in that house
made history
cooked banquets

partied with old friends
coked up
made new

choked up with ideas
changing the world
we were different, dammit

We chased out the roaches
the rats, stray cats, peeping toms
scavenging dogs

the pissing pregnant woman
who thought the place
abandoned

In that house
we grew together
into two adults who knew

the house was falling down
and we still laughed when the ceiling
collapsed in the lounge room

even when the electricity couldn't be bothered
to make its way to all the rooms
we held on

when most lights stopped working
showering by candlelight
we called it romantic

I was writing by soft lamps
with extension cords running
room to room to room

an indoor octopus
tentacles forcing electricity
to provide for us

The garden grew
more and more wild
encroaching upon the house

vines worked their way through the brickwork
until we showered and watered it
at the same time

mortar disintegrated
so it appeared only sand held
the bricks together

or we did

Until you told me
that within these sacred walls
you had betrayed me

I wandered those dark damp rooms
and wondered where
how many times

here on the kitchen bench
like some smutty porn scene
where I'd created false masterpieces

here where we racked up coke
and believed we would be invincible
because we were different, dammit

there where the ceiling caved in
over our dog
who somehow survived

here on a futon on the floor
where you and I had slept
because I was afraid

that with such intense wind
at the back of the house
our bedroom would become airborne

I made you leave that house
you packed your bags and boxes
took away half our home

Without 'us' filling it
it was impossible to romanticise
its impending demise

      That house rotted faster
      once you'd left, quickly it became so decrepit
      I could stand in some rooms

and stare up at the sky
even on a clear day
it would still be wet inside

      I loved that house

even as glass started falling
out of windows, shards sat splintered
outside and in

      even as doors started
      rusting on their hinges
      so I couldn't close them

even as dust started collecting
faster than I could remove it
even as the soft whiff of gas

      became frighteningly frequent
      even as the outside oasis
      tried to swallow the whole place

I still loved that house

>I got the call four months after you'd left
>they were pulling it down
>they were building something new

without the blemish of history
fancy, bigger, better, clean
rendered walls, smooth surfaces

>I had to leave
>take the remaining things
>through the poisoned bamboo forest

I moved just across a gully
the house squatted empty
perched forlorn on the edge

>insides gutted
>like a terminal illness
>had triumphed

I had a good view across
the chasm, and when it happened
I watched them tear it down

>It took them eight days
>to destroy everything
>removed every trace

The roof went first
then the outhouse
then all the outer walls

> then its insides
> then its foundations
> they went in with cranes and skips

I was angry
watching little men in hard hats
and high vis vests

> desecrate, remove, bury us
> with their machines
> and misguided ideas

of new

...

// Let's call it art //

// Stars drip liquid night sky / into her vision / she blinks back black eyes / moving blood in her mouth / rolling it around / spitting red / running tongue over stories / swollen like bleeding gums / she leaks ink like no other / it gushes / stained little rivers / she is lost in these criss-crossed lines / trace them with your gaze / already heavy / with what you want / you're simply method actors / with one take / She offers no salvation / ask her lovers / who sought some discovery / in empty fucking / there is no such thing / as innocent loving //

// Those colours are colossal / the immeasurable terrain unfamiliar / uneven beneath her feet / she is riddled with emotion / infested with anger / distorted by perversion / gravity gnaws at her / won't let her take off / nibble away fucker / she's gonna get so high / that even the gods / will be looking up at her / claiming she never knew madness / just the sadness / of unending unrequited love //

// She is moving with a body / which begs for forgiveness / from digressions from lucidity / (as though being human weren't madness amplified) / nobody can hear this / can't bear the thought of it / what their ears assemble instead / is the confidence of someone / who knows what's coming next / she collects each breath as a measurement / filling limitless cups to drink from / she pretends to(o) //

// Her blood has no cells / she embraces ego / knows that luminaries fill her blood stream / travelling through her heart / she is circling light / circumnavigated by night / chemicals taste best when self-medicating / life is a hard pill to swallow //

// It's breathing down her neck again / smells it fetid and foul / thumping fists against her breast / hammering home shit she can't know / she clasps narcissism to her chest / cuts secrets with scissors / makes confetti blizzards / watches the ink come back in rivers / these feelings won't wither / instead manipulated into mirrors / the figures she dances with / stepping on toes / tempts her with the sort of shit / she wants to be done with //

// It's a requirement / of the successful artist / to forget what it is / to be humble / so / she's immortal in the mortified kind of way / in the way Eve is / retold over and over / until everyone believes it //

// Come take these stories out of her mouth / relieve her of the swelling / come be a witness / remove the regrets / from that empty loving / she's making progress / moving away from the constant excesses / compassion and forgiveness / she's the other coming / until those colours suffocate / she's walking the streets / near enough to be here / just keep watching her suffer //

//

she said

she spoke of the finite
i was busy tapping
on typewriter keys
wasn't listening

thought she said infinite
didn't realise she was rehearsing
the ending

love has so many of those
i thought there were more
beginnings

i'm always surprised
when we get there
to where words are worthless

when drowning
they are weights
that make me sink quick

where my heart and breath
compete to see
which is fastest

i used to think
i echoed because i was hollow
she said / you reverberate
– it's different

the reverberations
got to be
too much for her

when i ride my motorbike
the vibrations are an amazing sensation
until without warning it overwhelms

she said / you never sit still
as though serenity
would get me out of this mess

i keep moving
because i'm afraid of inertia
wanting to stop
not being able to

at least this way
it's my choice
she rolled me a cigarette and said / here

where? / i asked
i felt a burning in my chest
i hadn't inhaled yet

sometimes seeds sprout
in the strangest places
my aortic pot plant
knows all about it

stuff grows
i'm no good at felling anything
she said / you've got to cut them down

you mean out / i replied
no, down
will it make a sound? / i asked

well that depends – are you present? /
only sometimes /
when I'm really focusing
on consciously existing

slipping between fantasies
has always been easy for me
you're never here / I've got work to do /
you're never here

i feel the immenseness of the universe
it's incessant
sitting between shoulder blades
scales balancing

it won't always be just us /
she said
why? / i asked

because this here's a moment /
how long does a moment last? /
a moment / she winked

i used to believe in forever
as though it were a tangible paradigm
aware of the paradox
i thought that's just how poets lived

time doesn't exist /
she said
still i constructed great monuments
to mark its passing

what is it? / she asked
it's a found poem / i said
is it dust? /

yes / i replied
it was created
when our bodies moved together

she rolled it up
placed it in my tear ducts
you cry too much / she said

i like sand
the sensation of it
under my feet
running through my fingers

a fist full
counting grains is a good way
to measure depth of feeling

the tide's coming in / she said
it just went out / i replied
it's going to be a tsunami /

she said and smiled

...

the i I was

With

ragged breaths and beating heart I ask you to 'make me new'. With careful eyes, lips, hands which will not miss those parts most in need, I ask you to understand that when I hide you must find me – something has stolen the i I was and now i am lost. Wordlessly, simply, with pleading eyes and sacred movements that our bodies know intuitively, I ask you to help me be reborn after that small death where I come to you again only to move away for I fear the being within – if you find me, know that something has stolen the i I was and now i am lost. My desperate pleas are barely hidden within these craving eyes: I ask you to bare yourself to me so that I will not fear my own nakedness – a naked and bloodied babe might stand before you, shaking, yes it's how you'll find me and you'll know that something has stolen the i I was and now i am lost. How will I be found? Through your skin? The scent of us on sheets smeared already with something like the longing for tears? I dare not cry until emptied, then it will be all I can shed. I'll ask you to give for I'll have nothing left yet every reason to live except these thoughts which tell tales, tempting some inner enemy in me. So find me. On you. Within you. Searching, for what has stolen

...

Tangled

desire wraps itself
around our throats like rope
and we choke

what words could be whispered
are restricted to gasps
that escape

we can trace
some tracks towards
our potential demise

but lack the vision
to avoid
those oncoming collisions

for we are gods
driven not by the divine
but by more earthly delights

products of the breeding construct
except we neither inseminate
nor create new beings

we are new beings
ourselves
reborn in a form

vile to some
rapturous to us
we are willing to consummate

that state that leaves morals
prostrate
and the ego inflated

laying waste to wanting
no matter how obstinate
there are plenty more

willing to traverse this landscape
where sweat and tears intermingle
from years of avoiding the substantial

by focusing instead between legs
and sheets
needs

get tangled in
breath
gets tangled in

hedonism
gets tangled in
unwanted emotion

gets tangled in
lies
gets tangled in

the selfless
gets tangled in
the selfish

the greedy
the giving
the unforgiving

drawing life from an act
that's drawing life
from the unliving

.

yes we are gods
but we have forsaken
what it is to be sublime

instead
we wield a knife
for fleshy crimes

we carve into ourselves
into our skin
we sin

without harp
or song
we cannot sing

whilst our mouths are filled
with words
brandishing intent to hurt

we fuck
as though our bodies
could save the world

.

though we can't save ourselves
from our desperate needs
getting tangled in breath

our only way to avoid death
getting tangled in
hedonism that never ends

getting tangled in
unwanted emotion
for we lack the ability

to honestly process
getting tangled in
lies that we tell ourselves

trying to placate
the voice that states
the truth

getting tangled in
the selfless
those others

the victims
getting tangled in
the selfish us

the greedy us
the giving the lost
the barely living

and we
the unforgiving

...

Braying beasts

I am seeking sanctuary or solace
in the skin and kisses of strangers
searching for some sense of the surreal
as an escape from reality

I remain solitary
swimming in the scent of sex
and its total lack of sentiment
fist deep in primitive pleasings

knowing that once again
I have over spent
in the hope that
I might find respite from these nights

where thoughts of such impurity
are better played out
than kept as seeds germinating –
fantasies that cannot be uttered

I am searching for an epigraph
an obituary on their flesh
in their breath
so that with some knowledge

I might stave off these little deaths
a while longer
I am the hunger that flashes
the teeth that gnash

one part of the beasts
that bray with bared teeth
collide with bodies so hard
the clash is like lightning

the ascent climbing heights
only hedonistic seekers of delight
might comprehend
we are the flames of a fire

that appear to proclaim
'free me from the constraints of my being'
so that skyward we might stretch
until into our limbs are etched

things the universe has kept from us
things we will now keep from others
there are words I dare not utter
I am listening to every breath

sitting beneath the din of these
exasperated longings
impatiently sifting through
doubled over bodies

bending to be bruised
begging to be used
believing we are lost
though through corridors

we thrust
hoping that by touch
we might find some hidden divinity
or at least a soliloquy

to explain what I've hidden here
- an aside where I admit
there is no denying
I am trying to fill a hole

so cavernous
that even fingers in mouths
cannot fill it
nor can they find them

the words
if they did
they would slip and fit like rings
then the world would see

I am simply seeking to be lost
then found
I will sketch my story
on your aching body

and hope what is hidden
can be freed for a short while
I will plead for you to beg
demand you not to stop

I will be heavy upon you
you will feel life
from my heat
I will cry tears that tell of broken fantasies

you will carry my burden
for the time it takes us
to lock eyes and breathe short rasps
then we will disconnect

I will leave heavier in the knowledge
that what I sought
and thought I'd found
I have lost again

...

I will be a God without you

I laid at your feet...kissed your swollen toes and ankles...begged you to keep walking on me...told you I was desperate to let you in...a masochist...willing to douse this fire inside...as long as I wasn't forced to look any longer in your mirror

You were a burden...a cross to bear...but fuck you were sexy...sexier than Jesus...so sexy it was all he could talk about...crucified with guilt through the wrists...remorse through the feet...still swollen

I stood in your shadow...called it your shade...bellowed into your crevices...heard you echoed back to me...believed in you...listened when you called...you promised me a place where hallmark cards were no longer written...a world where I could sit on my own throne...the Queen of Hearts...my loyal subjects bowing before me...beings beating back at me

You hurled your beauty at me...I caught it unquestioningly...with fingers already bent out of shape from being broken too many times...trying to wrangle the massive...for those who couldn't handle it all...cracked and splintered hands...from having clutched at ugliness too long...nails bitten down in moments of fear that others...who had tried to claw it out of me...had won

They had...now you sit in the pit of my stomach...grow like cancer...you spread through me until I am diseased with you... rotting from the inside out...I am on all fours begging you to sodomise me...this hole in my heart is an opening you see...I'm not missing anything...come in...get comfortable...you and me need to get better acquainted...with a shot gun...a bottle of rum

Come, let's move you from my sleeve...up to my forehead...you will be the stamp...the tattoo...that lets people know you are inside me...I am infused with you...you sit in my bowels...even if I wished it I couldn't shit you out...

Should someone say your name...I will tell them it sounds ugly in their mouths...people do bad things in your name...you're an excuse...a pitiful thing people use to break all the rules

Before...I would have bled for you...I would have sustained the worst types of pain for you...there's no wound I would have refused for you...I would have slit these wrists...placed kisses on lips of the emotionally diseased...said...'come bleed with me'

You were a shaman, a sham...and when I declared it...people told me it would just take time...I slit their throats...watched them bleed to death...whilst telling them 'It'll just take time'...see what you've done to me

I would have shed layers of skin until only bone was left...would have fed the earth with my entrails...metres of intestines laid out in the shape of the letters that spelled your name...but you wouldn't let me in...you teased me like some little slut using their body as a commodity...you were intent on dangling a carrot to make this donkey follow...

I surfed cosmic currents where time no longer mattered for you...I created crutches out of poems...so that even legless...half dead...I could still stand up for you...crossed seasons of disbelief...

navigated oceans of human tears...tested reason...only to come to the conclusion...gravity is a mad man-made illusion...just like sanity...so whilst I stood on the roots of trees...reaching for the sun...drowning in sky's blue...I declared heaven and hell to be two forms of the same...

you

I have stood and faced death for you...grasping rusty razor blades in gritty hands...poised above lies and deceit...ready to carve truths from them...I have held that poisoned chalice to my lips...as you entreated me to drink of you holding nose and breath...I took you into me...all the way down my throat...until I was gagging on you...even with my mouth full I said...

'can you hear me mother fucker? rain down on me...give me what you've got...I'll take all of it!...without it I couldn't belong here... not of this earth...where stained with the shame of being your fool...I have cried into pillows...stuffed with feathers plucked from liar birds...I have dried my eyes on the cloth of what was lost... cursed upon every breath that denied me death'...

Let me lay on your bed of nails...demand you stand upon me... so I may then count the pinpricks of my own expiration...You made me a victim...Where once I was a lion my roar is a purr lost in your sizeable silence...I will become numb to you...I will resist your tempting call...your siren's cry...I will stab you dead where you once resided...I will be deaf and blind to your signals and signs...no longer will I climb onto all fours...

Fuck you...murderer...serial killer...killer of every fairy tale...every fable...you spread and smother...suffocate...you are the end of all things beautiful...you tempt with ridiculous tricks of light...flights of fancy...seducing me into self-loathing...you get under the skin of your hosts...

I will not be one of those...no...I will not be one of those...I discard you as nothing more than an empty word...uttered by desolate beings....you are my enemy...I am yours....

...

Sariñena: an ending, for now

1.

Church bells peal across the dusk sky
echo off colours reflected
deepened by desert dust
a beautiful sound made jarring
symbolic of a countdown

storks in their nests
bury their beaks in their chest
gather on the steeple
as they preen each other
settle to rest

each ring denotes time passing

2.

We have elected to lock ourselves in
a confinement self-inflicted
metal shutters
transforming our room
into a dark den of expression

late afternoon heat
fingers window seals
threatening to find entry
a cantankerous air conditioner
wheezes as it fights back

this lethargic battle moves around us
we are aware only
of our own oblivion

and the attrition of time

3.

I am carving questions
into your skin with my tongue
burying my nose in your armpits
seeking some resolve from your scent

hands cupped beneath buttocks
wringing justification from flesh
investigating with my palms
extracting explanations

from your movement
pleading with you to provide
just one reason why we can't exist
despite physical distance

I imagine I can span
the impending separation
with my hands
these finger tips

press into bruises
my lips and teeth have made
your surface scores easily
wears its responses with certainty

I want to mark your whole body
make it a reflection
of the desert dusk sky
experiencing vertigo

will I topple, or will I dive

4.

No one has ever
met my stare
the way you do

we hold, hold,
eyes locked
something surges from my guts

those bells peal through my chest
I am forced to look away first
often there are sounds

that echo out my mouth
before I can silence them
the storks ruffle their feathers

settle

5.

Every meal is a beautiful trial
decoding menus in our broken Spanish
legs pressed together beneath the table
dipping *pan* in *aceite de oliva*

working our way through the
menu del dia
drinking *agua con gas*
sharing *postres*

already we have devised
our own language
secret tongues
in the way we lean

cock our heads
curl our lips
tuck hair behind ears
we can't wait to escape

back to our nest
where without the fever of our bodies
the air conditioner
chilled heat's crusade

an exercise in patience

6.

The deeper we dive / the tighter the fit / we quicken our breath
/ fight submit commit to memory / through wet spit blood teeth
/ grit buck seethe fuck / brace split come we come / we come we
come we come / we come breathe shudder / unable to resist / the
desert has found its way inside / the ceiling is a dusk sky / your
breath / the feathers of storks on my face / I ache / pupils expand
swallow irises / with questions answered

our hearts chime
the bell tolls
lover it tolls
it tolls

we are out of time

7.

This exhausted waking
dragging my body into the shower
leaning against cool tiles
wanting the goodbyes over

I prefer the aching of separation
to the anxiety of an impending parting
dressing quickly
I need to leave

the train is barrelling towards us
our goodbyes feel stilted
strange, you smell like sleep still
we press lips, bodies

a quick tangle of standing limbs
we pull away
I'm turning, walking
receiving a blown kiss

Stepping outside
heat's not begun

I pause

Church bells peal across the dawn sky
echo off colours reflected
deepened by desert dust
a beautiful sound made jarring

symbol of an ending

...

Our new language (Maria the first)

Standing on the platform
at Central Station
nervous fidgeting
eyes darting

seeking your face out
amongst moving masses
there you are
rushing towards me

anxious smile I hug you tight
with a mouthful of hello
knowing the awkwardness of
three years of relative silence

would settle upon us quickly
it did
so I hug you again
willing myself to be present

        Instead
        I'm back in the car with you
        three years ago
        when silence stretched between forced

        syllables
        I was an arsehole
        who took away your agency
        made a liar out of me

broke your heart
I remember the way your voice splintered
how you reached out
I pulled back

turned inward
so deep
I couldn't see it
etched in us

Back on the platform
pulling away from our strange embrace
mouth full of everything unsaid
I see what you've managed to erase

what's been carved into me
I am aware of everything
too suddenly
willing myself to be present

Instead
I am somewhere in an alternative universe
where I could have been happy with you
could have loved you

for a really long time
if I hadn't been such a coward
my mouth is not full of anything now
it's dry as you ask about my flight

my thirty hours travelling
we find safety in the banal
I fill the air with similar noise
I can't look at you

all I want to do is look at you
actually all I want to do is kiss you
Three years of silence
all I want to do is kiss you

We are sitting in an empty library
books propped open
in a language I can't fathom
like our new language

so hard to navigate
I tell you I really like your partner
it's a lie I fucking hate them
they love you

like I was never able to
They remind me of me in many ways
I dislike my reflection in them
you tell me you've never felt more loved

in all your life
I want to apologise
take your hands
tell you I was so afraid back then

all the time
then press your lips against mine
beg you to forgive
everything I put you through

believe me to be a better being now
I don't
I just listen smile
will myself to be present

        Instead
        I'm back where you and I stood in a turret
        atop a castle
        in another country

        I was inside you
        your breath on my ear
        as you told me
        you could never ever refuse me

Here in the library
I am overcome by the need
to test whether
you can refuse me now

I tighten my fists into balls
push my nails into my palms
and let 'I'm happy for you, really I am'
tumble out my mouth over and over again

Later I tell you about how sick I've been
embarrassed tears run
I wipe them away hurriedly
telling you I never cry

both know that's a lie
you tell me to take my own medicine
be vulnerable for once
I talk of being a burden

you call me your friend
– never a burden
'friend'
who knew that word could cut so deep

three years of silence
you have moved me into friend
hearing your voice utter that
fills me with regrets which can not

tumble out of my mouth
You're happy
I'm happy for you
really I am it's just

                    I should have loved you
                    better back then

...

loss like you and she

she misses you ache chasm stretching
gorge deep hollow resounding running
the length of her fist clenching furrowed
brows tightening can't breathe inhale or

you cannot bear her loss she imagines
your own hidden alcohol numbed casual
sex delaying ruin dares not ask how you
hold others push grind fuck sigh o repeat

mornings hardest eyes flutter squeezing
sun through loose curtains stay sleeping
please heart compacting constricting her
thorax tightening lungs this pain physical

she counts days a cross through each on
a calendar unsure what she's marking off
losing time raw excruciating pressure just
here black marker stains on fingers cheek

you ask to speak soften the displacement
her body out of reach no curl press stretch
breath connect crave voice familiar sound
phone in hand like hand in hand closest to

she can't handle it requests silence desires
a schism trying to forget lips eyes toes arse
fingers soapy baths sleep-ins holding body
tight skimming skin dreams kissing of grins

she meanders through days lost in thought
memories fantasies of homecoming airport
intense joy circling arms rolling suitcase to
battered car still speckled with your red hair

you had an awful choice home or home her
or friends family familiar city history echoing
alleyways dancing down streets alive known
not lonely like before screaming loss at love

you're a different lonely missing her strength
ever holding believing speaking into your ear
how worthy you are of this her belief you can
forget so easily when she isn't repeating love

she's just trying to push through tonight netflix
numbed chocolate binge don't think she can't
think the brink beckoning like never before a
slippery darkness losing her footing gripping

your nights are different full lights dance floor
a grimy pub beer blunted not her body a bed
nowhere near the place you were together in
sacred fevered touch o amplification of ardour

eventually she succumbs slips between the
sheets allowing time for imagining spooning
whispers laughter pillow pushing biting gasp
tightening the crying it keeps getting worse o

when will this cycle of missing just end crash
collapse in upon itself this it takes time but of
course time takes what it takes no control so
heart craving body tightening future that was

you're lost too not enough to return to her yes
she knows but can't make her heart believe it
how over the two of you are still both adrift the
suffering ironic if you could hold one another o

the unending pain would end

...

Citadel of Sighs

I woke to our
bodies: already moving
limbs tangled breath tangled
eyes still closed
the sun not yet risen

Cold air danced on our skin
telling its own stories
we were listening
with: goosebumps
hairs that stood on end

I began to build a citadel out of sighs
so that you might realise
the true nature of this thing
Lifting our bodies towards the ceiling
we sought to find some sense

but ended up instead
in this surreal
discovering what it meant
to move until the sun
told the cold to stop speaking

so it might light up our bodies
and dust particles we were disturbing
There is liquid in your eyes
bees made their home nearby
created honey behind your pupils

I am sticky with your gaze
it sits inside me
while you whisper poetry
onto my flesh
making sentences fingers

I am reduced to
making grand statements about
you: the cosmos
me: a simple satellite
navigating time and space

to beat a little closer
to your rhythms
in order to send you
the right signals
lips breath

When I am not with you
you are still present
I walk with your memory
in my footsteps
accompanied by your scent

it sits on my lips
covers my fingers
whose tips tapped out
morse code on your body
things I simply couldn't say

like: our desire is the binding yarn
that seals the colourful tapestry
transporting feelings wordlessly
so that our bodies
can accept gifts graciously

we are praying
at some sort of altar here
no false idols feared
we will love less violently
so our citadel will:

sparkle shimmer shine
as we rediscover through skin
the sublime

...

love might be

unfinished sympathy plays on the car stereo as my eyesshouldersheart ache...the road opens up into highways like sliced arteries pouring cars into cities waiting to engulf them ready jawsopenwide a yawning metropolis that at least offers corners to hide()this is my massive attack()i have images in my mind of bluebrownblack polaroids that failed to develop unlike the bruises that would spot my body if emotions manifested so obviously()they were beautiful anyway those polaroids and somewhere in those haikus over which we argued whilst we ate tofu and smoked damiana i realised::this existence i have been swept into cannot run parallel()unlike these highways I now drive through()cut me down the middle split me open wide i will represent humanities current divide where blood may be one colour but not our binding force::we create only to suffer::free thoughts form on these freeways where the mind wanders i wonder back to timesplaces()i tried to lay claim to a people only to be told we are all equal her with the wrong colour skin teaching me lessons about humanity's forked tongue with sting::how little I know...please tell me you can see what I'm willing to give up—this sacrifice...()some small insignificant offering()...i will argue we are earth's parasite and through our lives by our very existence we seek only to take to accumulate— earth our host we here to suck it dry...you might say it's too radical...you over there might say it's possible...sometimes i want to retract my words bindthemswallowthem so they can't enter the atmosphere add to the negative energy but instead i'll say::love might be the only reason we exist::the only thing that separates us from monstrous beasts certainly not the ability to reason or ask intelligent questions for the majority of us does neither...we are entering the city i have relinquished control of the steering wheel my lids were too heavy i slumber lightly windscreen wet with water dropping from night time skies sky scraper lights blurring into soft yellows and whites::I must confess::there's not much left in me with which to fight

...

there is no poetry left in me today

last night i sketched
a dozen sonnets
into your wanting

that's 168 lines
i pressed into your skin
with mine

kissed ode
after ode
upon your lips

told you
what i hoped
would be our story

with the movement
of my hips

...

Impermanent

Those whispers that were present
and fell like feathers onto the bed
we should never have laid in together
wept their own secrets onto sheets
of minimum thread

Restricted totally by the binds we
roped round the sounds our mouths made
to halt longings not meant to be uttered
we held back just enough
so those lives we couldn't have lived forever

didn't intrude on this
impermanent heaven of never
Had you bothered asking for honesty
I would have answered honestly:
truth is not my forte

so should you lay with me
know when you submit
it is to small offerings
the tumult of bodies
in the tangle of sheets

those constant reminders to breathe
are all you're going to get
whatever is hidden
remains so for a reason
it's not for either of us to dig

know we can never trade
this piece of small for something big

...

X

You are aware of only breath
       the impending tempest
somewhere lies an island
       you are heading for it

what marks the spot
       stolen treasures calling you
it glitters this gold
       which was sold into slavery:

the heart learning to beat
       sails raised at half mast
who is the ship
       when truth is the storm

you cannot find the holy grail
       if you have less virtue
than the angels
       you denounce

o heart o creature that
       moves in the chest
pressing against lungs
       you restrict breath

when breath is what is needed most
        what marks the spot
where you gather yourself
        to go on

...

Without it almost nothing

The spines of books
digging into our skin
I feel them pressing in as we kiss
this joining of multiple loves
intellectual divine

The hot mess of your sex
panting pressing wet
black lines on white pages
neat and tidy between hard
tangible covers more solid than us?

It's better not to get existential
while sheets are getting twisted
I've resisted these thoughts before
when the sun was filtering through
the stained glass of our tiny house

the currawongs were dipping their beaks
in the compost heap
striking worm gold
Every time I've repelled these thoughts
I've eventually come back

rappelling down that hare hole of fear
at losing this us this brilliant unbridled us
which could give that stained glass a run for its money
where we spiritualise sensuality
incense burning oil heating

we forget about this
often bleak situation
we've been thrust into

> On that dance floor when we first met
> I told you I was a poet
> you spoke about the power of language
> to give voice to those parts of us most integral
> how without it we're almost nothing

Almost

> That night we got high
> danced until sweat drenched
> our feet ached
> we collapsed onto your mattress
> found more energy again

Now we push the books
off the edges of our bed
as we push each other
to the edges of ourselves
repelling the finite once more

ignoring the sound of it knocking
above the currawong calls

...

what this is

free fall slow
into your curves

rest my head
between your hip and ribs

tiny hairs connect
with my lips

hand spread over your belly
trying to think less

about all the what if-s
all the could be-s

watching the rise and fall
of your chest

fingers in your hair
needing to know

...

safety is this

Morning::
rain tip-toes across
the tin roof
eyes
still closed
she inhales her

Awaken::
she's in that darkness before waking
unconsciously remembers its space
to float not suffocate
don't dream away the light baby

Open::
eyelashes dance sleepily
with a yawn she says
/ sometimes waking makes
me feel limbless /
she replies
/ we're weightless together /
corner of mouth twitches
to grin
kiss morning breath kiss
/ you're so cheesy lover /

Invaded::
Her body is a
desecrated temple
she's trying to rebuild
looks in the mirror
disfigurement from breast to pubic bone
how can she be loved like this: scarred

Easy::
words waver when
she is brimming with colour
/ let me paint my love
across every mark /
draws her away from the mirror
/ you are the sum of different parts /

Sea storm::
the dark ocean broils like witches' potions
boiling in scalding cauldrons
she throws her words
casting spells with tears
her heart and wounds
thrusts them deeper into the water
cries out loud
/ why do you do this /
/ what did I do
to deserve this /

Respite::
at night you join again
laughter a healing salve
moonshine on a still sea
curve of arm in hip
safety is this

Night::
sinking deep into mattress
existence's unbearable burden
dissipates weightlessness again
the two of them
curled around each other
their dreams playing like movies
imagine you can see
energy dazzling electric fluorescent incandescent

3am::
breath REM spread fingers
twitch sleep talk soft sensation
of loss lost in the unknowable
watch them reach for each other
even in the deepest sleep
this doesn't last forever
every love eventually severed
right now though
they're bound together

...

incensed

I could smell her nag champa
burning when she walked out
small plastic bag of belongings
banging against her leg I yelled
/ You don't fucking know how to
be loved / at her back collapsed
tears packed against eyeballs o
overflow taste of salty sweet on
my lips where the imprint of her
                    last kiss still singed

...

not another love poem

This isn't another love poem
emptied as I've been by the world's ache
every atlas a tome of violent suffering

geography a lesson uncovering
arbitrary lines absolutely dissimilar
to human connection

It's impossible to write about the
kissing of lips stroking of skin
two bodies talking in the tongue of

dreams when brutality seems
the universal language How can I
write about the sensation

of you and me in the night
hands clasped bodies tight
when colonialists are experiencing

what the colonised have been living:
blownupthroatsslitdrivenovergunneddown
shotupbodiessplitviolentlonersineverytown

more reasons to poison the people
justifying unprecedented carnage
it's too jarring like uttering your name

with only love on my lips whilst witnessing
images of children's bodies broken and twisted
nothing more than UN statistics lover

to write about your eyes how they bore into
mine so I've nowhere to hide free fall
into your embrace covering my face

with your hands to try to block out the sight
of every news source every horror story
every gory unrelenting detail

witnessing the pouring of refugees
across borders being blocked
Refugees the visual manifestations

of our species' dysfunction
I want to speak about love
in a way everyone understands

the type between two people
who have shown each other their demons
the crazy teeming just beneath the surface

how it doesn't make them worthless
I just can't write another love poem though
but one beyond the narrative of just two

about our capacity and ability
to love consciously without condition
expectation derision demands

evolving beyond tribes oppressing
slaughtering obliterating creating divides
stripping humanity of its human rights

I can't shake this feeling I need to write
another poem about love as a form of resistance
because right now it seems the world

has forgotten love's existence

...

we have become a museum of intangible things

I realise this
as we skype again

now I'm learning
to gild a cage for my tongue

I have learnt
not to speak truth

To hear it echoed back
from your void splinters me

You speak like water
gushing out a faucet

or sand gripped
in slippery hands

Now we're less than
the more we were

There is a haze
in your language

you talk westerlies
while I sit in the east

My tongue tests the bars
proud they resist (barely)

your breath catches the tail
of your chatter

we pause
stare at computer lenses

closest to locking eyes
across continents

I'm tempted
to break out my tongue

for its own moment
of absolute

but realise it's not you
I'm talking to it's you

so while you speak shadows
I imprison my tongue

I can't say I love you
I fear to stop loving you

else this emptiness
loses its purpose

if we're really history
where does that leave me

…

livinthefinite

I wanted to love her until her bones ached
until her marrow knew only my name

I wanted to love her with nothing more than my ears
so that she knew I really was hearing every word and
insinuation all those things left unsaid so she didn't even
need to speak when she thought I was deaf

I wanted to slice off both my ears offer them to her
on a platter she had woven from forgiveness and say
        / take them / both of them /

/ keep them in your pockets so I can hear you /
/ even when I'm not near you /
/ what use do I have for these anyway /
/ if not to listen to your heart beat /

I wanted to love her so that she would never know need
so that in this labyrinthine consuming desire
        I would know exactly what she wanted when

and be able to express it with nothing more than my skin
I wanted to love her so that she would never know sadness
again so that in those moments where her hammering heart
made it hard for her to breathe I could do more than just

kiss away her tears I could remove the very tear ducts from
her eyes place them in mine say / I will shed this brine /
         / you need only float /

/ buoyed by the fact there is someone in this world /
/ who will cry for you /
/ there is someone in this world /
/ who will cry for you /

I wanted to love her so much she knew what it was to
transcend time place the physical restraints of being
         restricted to living in skin so she would be a god

divine in her own right more powerful than even the one
people pray to on knees begging for the forgiveness
they know they will never receive I would purge her
of her own guilt murmur: / by absolutely no rights /

/ vested in me as just another fucking lost child of this universe /
/ I absolve you / you don't need to carry anything /
         / not even me /

I wanted to love her in a way she'd never been loved
before with pure adulation in adoration so when she looked
into me she would see that love emanating constantly yes this
is the insanity with which I wanted to love her fists at the ready

to fight beat back this broken world tell it to leave us alone
I wanted to love her within our inner secluded spaces
covert under cover in case
                anyone tried to wrangle this love away from us

I wanted to love her before our wounded histories
unpacked their sickly symphonies and played out our songs for us
I wished to inscribe into our flesh these very words
so that the raised imprints would be scar tissue
we could run our fingers over a private brail only we knew

        she wanted to be loved
        without the violence

that meant without the depth of wells dug before my birth
before the birth of my parents before the birth of theirs
before before before before before
I just wanted to be loved without the suspicion

        there was always some other
        in my meaning

I clearly couldn't love her without the delirium she invoked
so we choked on misunderstandings even as I battled
the way these delusions belittled our magnificent empire
we shrunk into nothing more than wrong words
flung from exasperated tongues
                placed in the palms of our hearts

I wanted to love her as only I know how to love which is
to love until that love becomes a carcass
buried beneath the rubble of a thousand try agains
        she wanted to love forever even if the form changed

at least now I can tell you what's better

…

tag

i want to graffiti your skin
paint you with intent
tag my name all over your body

with my breath
design a mural on your flesh
with my fingertips and lips

feel you resist
just a bit
leave fading imprints with my teeth

not the type that bruise
just those that mark for seconds
then disappear

impermanence is
scrawled stories
over your curves

i will be the ink that writes
along your contours
until you clench

release
breathe

...

Julian(n)

you shimmer
it's all I can see
when I look at you
a sort of shimmering
it's too easy to compare
you to the sea:
expansive
unknown
   inherently known
I want to swim
in your waters
just to know you
a little
one salty drop at a time
I'm a strong swimmer
I feel like you should know
I can also float
for hours at a time
stare up at the sky
watch clouds gather
subside
feel your waters rise
I don't know you
   I know you
it could all be an illusion
   Atlantis - you could be Atlantis

I'm a strong swimmer
I feel like you should know
I can also float
for days at a time

...

Well, know this

I am seeking something sacred
from between her lips
where tongue pushes past breath
to simultaneously seduce and defend

She runs it along the ridge of my ear
then whispers things – secrets
we lovers of love have fought to protect
by loving in the hardest places placing love
in the palms of strangers the hearts of haters

introducing ideas to the contemplators
ignoring those who would try to persuade us
that love is for the weak
would try to dissuade us
from being able to love
in a way that defeats

For now I am lost in the poetry we are creating
through each other sketching it across our bodies
I swear to write wings into her back
so that she can flee if we begin to sink
saying things like 'forever at the moment'
as wind to keep her airborne

born into a lovelessness
that's hard to understand I cut beneath that thin skin
and whisper into wounds that love
doesn't have to be sick it doesn't have to be sick

I wake in a night so thick
trees are frozen
animals have ceased to shriek

but the ocean is still calling me
the score the backdrop to her hands
on my body running my length
eyelashes to breasts
centre to thighs toes

this happens most nights – I think
she's searching for something
I don't know if I've got it or maybe
I've got it all wrong and she's not looking
for anything instead she's mapping out
the contours of our new love

maybe she's plotting the spots
we need to travel maybe I could be her world
and she an adventurer
not a coloniser – discovering – not conquering

Ours is a landscape without borders
or definitions where we understand
all forms of fences as defence from infiltration
are fabricated out of phantoms
seeking to keep love out
I want love to be in here sitting inside our bodies
beating every rhythm of our heart beats for us

believing in the subconscious
seeking something beyond this
we come to conclusions that would make
even the most violent gods weep –
they would understand
we know how to love better than them
every truth we seek will be a statement
to those who would deny our love
call it something unreal unequal

Well, know this: I will always love with every atom
every part of my being every piece of matter
That static which lights up each caress
is evidence that love is bigger
than the human disease
of denying love where it should be

...

This is my wish

I've always felt like some sort of super human super lover
untouchable in the confines of the worlds I have created for us
lying on my back staring up at clouds I am not seeing shapes
I am seeing your eyes shadowing them sifting through these
hallucinations knowing my rumination will lead only to the
ruination of our empire **I am touching blue** touching grey
touching neither of us blinking back light rays heating up my
pupils blinding me with a light too bright I hide behind sunglasses
they are commas before each sentence **at the end of each breath**
where words die only a little death before being brought back
to life after that moment we allow ourselves a slice of **silence
to gather** ammunition or strength or what is left in the air but
space that remains tainted already by **threats of you leaving**
I'M LEAVING I'M LEAVING I'M FUCKING WALKING
AWAY WEAVING PAST TABLES AND CHAIRS AND
CONVERSATIONS THEY'RE ALL LIES MOST OF THE
TIME THESE FUCKING CONVERSATIONS **TRYING TO
FILL** THE IMMEASURABLE MISERABLE VOID weaving
past tables chairs conversations they're all lies most of the time
those conversations filling a vacant vapidity oh god fuckit here
is the issue **my love and life** I can miss you I can miss you as
though you were a limb and you haunt me as a phantom for my
tears are panting tired from the constant drip leaky eyes leaking
past sunglasses **each extrication** drop it drips onto the pieces of
me you used to kiss the pieces of me now strung together with
only string the pieces of me that once were **the points of us**
where that string could gather and tell the story of our past but
past these past the point of believing anymore past the walking
of streets until I am tired exhausted waiting for **time to recede**

how can it my mind peals through an infinite weariness time is a loop that plays over and over like an ear worm a song I can't stand my feet pad upon pavement also **wanting a moment** of respite tired from bearing the brunt the fall of my footsteps I promise not to step on your cracks pavement you must promise not to let my lover break my back pavement I want **to forget the imprint** of every footstep I have left in this life so far and every footstep I have weathered I am stamped with love the lack and abundance of afraid that **the rhythm of my hurt** will play on and on like that goddamn ear worm I want to forget the feel of all of you on me and the sound of my footsteps pleading with the night to let me be let me sleep eventually I do and will but not soundly with **a reoccurring dream** in this nightmare I know what others don't – a tsunami is coming I tell all who will listen and run that slow run of sleep trying to escape but it bears down upon **me I hope to float** waking in sweats I hope to be healed I wish to rejoin this world live in it move in it strain against the resistance of it get lost in it THIS IS MY WISH I may as well **wish for wings** for tingling skin to be kissed for my back to be stroked for whispers of what once was I want to rise like that famed phoenix or I will float I will float upon you and be our saviour deny death its right to life deny the ending too soon of something that should **breathe** yet we are cut from all that came before fashioned by all that should come now more we exist in some form of transparency that the whole **universe** can see through we are smoke and mirrors we are glass and every form of unravelling I ever envisaged required you as the spool to wrap me up again to wrap me up again **come wrap me up again** coming undone in this fashion leaves me with too many loose ends which will only stop once I reach this

precipice this balancing point this thing we believed in this lover is
me this lover is **the end of me** blinking in the darkness of what
once was my light searching for what looking for what something
that tells me we must **push on**

...

prohibited

With their bodies intertwined it's so easy
to deny what she really wanted
she can convince herself
this is enough to fill the hollowness
their bodies pressed firmly
every curve filled with the other
so easy to deny every caress scarring marking
reminders of these prohibited moments

she needs more nothing has been filled
in fact extra has been emptied
lord knows she has nothing to spare
there are parts of her scattered
both of them torn in tatters stripped bare
still neither can be dissuaded from going there

this was never going to be guilt free
it doesn't matter truth can't be doctored only masked
the mistress carries her burden of knowing
which is always the other woman's fate
someone somewhere blissfully unaware
their lover is a low down lying cheat

but it's not for nothing
see this love may be a hidden malignant growth
but for only two who know it's there
it resounds loud like a constant beat
in the tone of unspoken boom

There are stains on the bed which will remain
the sheets unwashed for days on end
just so that smell can trigger memories
fleeting turning to something melancholic –
they are still hers they are the scent of skin on skin
where the pleadings should have been *leave me be*
but were *fuck you and this and us*
why is this what makes me free
when you're never going to leave

she is powerless even though the movement of their bodies
empowers both of them it's the most powerful they've ever felt
together they discover pleasures
she holds her lover's desires in her fingers mouth inner sanctum
exerting her will submitting beneath it
knowing she is the reason for every sharp intake of breath
pleading moan groan between dry parted lips
every drop of wet every small death rebirth again death rebirth

repeat These were their moments heavy in meaning
no matter how fleeting the whole experience
comparative to lives lived these were their moments
vulnerable imminent goodbyes
impending emptiness overcoming them
promises made they know each will break
making noises about this always being
an exercise in futility destined to end
considering infidelity is not honesty's fertile ground

one last time they lie side by side only pinkies touching
soft exhausted smiles sweat spots their foreheads
the space between their breasts
the concave parts of their lower backs
where the body dips before flourishing from hips
speaking in murmurs about parts of their lives
up till now hidden speaking about desires beyond the flesh
this night theirs they own it they know it
seeking each other out again sleepily languidly
until the sun rises

when each are worlds away distant through time and space
they both occasionally relive those moments
knowing if people had deciphered their coded little love life
it would have sullied and demonised
their foray into unlawful love
but for all their lies and secrecy
all the time they lost every act of indecency
they still believe in this their history

...

I can't just switch it off

Part I

We were imbued
with a sacredness
that infused us
a sensation
of moving with the universe
one force of energy
touch created illumination
shadows like illusions sweeping
white spaces with figures
enacting out on walls
what our bodies were formed for

exaltations expressed through
exhalations dripping then drenched
a medley of
heavy caresses
played out in a melody
at high volume
we intoned with voices
greater than our own
a new state of being
with exuberance we shifted
away from our humanness

We were visions to each other
couched in an elation
that comes from

bodies connected to some
things we could never understand
we cannibalised one another
devoured our longings
consumed the burning
then lit fires beneath
the thirst so that it evaporated
returned
dissolved again

Part II

That cycle still sits within me
without the relief of our bodies colliding
I spin
whilst the cravings spread
knowing that this period of enlightenment
has ended

If I cannot gorge myself on you
fill myself to full
I am left starving
a forced fasting
malnourished from trying
to exist on the memories alone
of how I devoured your extremities
before entering
inhaled your cries
pushed past your pain

I was the flame that licked
at every fragment
left you burning
until you turned into smoke
filling my room
an invisible vapor
that whirled with the incense we burnt
spirals entangled as our
bodies' shadows were

Part III

You don't want to know
about my suffering
the passion was okay
when you were in love with me
but suddenly this other side is ugly

Unfortunately I can't just switch it off
I have not regained my humanness
I am still that animal
seeking the scent of you
on sheets pillows
my t-shirts you wore
one whiff
and I am overcome by despair
at this finality

it's a form of masochism
I sit and witness my own sickness
not interested in self forgiveness

So come back to me
for one last fuck
we'll make it just that
shed our skins
leave multiple trails of
blood sweat tears
smeared on sheets
that are the final page
of our story
I want nothing to do with your heart
just your body
let's cheapen the whole experience
we'll make it a transaction
your flesh for my sanity
I don't care if this vulgar state
leaves you disgusted
because there are parts of me
grotesque
I recede into these
find them comforting
in these moments
of ugly unabashed wanting

...

I tread this coastal path

I know you
through this
coastal path

tread summer
times we were
                    electric

enervated
incensed
the sea a salve

throwing shapes into the sky
white wash trashed
against rocks

dipping deep as
upturned mountains
I know you

against the azure
a silhouette in polaroids
overexposed

                    we laughed
colonised
exotified browns

against
paler shades of privilege
our joke

alone

the winter glare
barely bearable

hood over hat over sunglasses
warding off wind
standing

        on the edge of

stone lips
great yawning waters

stepping down to safety
we are
embedded in this path

beneath my sandy feet
in the concrete
on the lisp of a breeze

the wheeze of a calmer sea
beneath the drying   **wings**
of a resting cormorant

spread outstretched

        we are

...

Edge Sky Self

She's a ruined mountain
heart scar tissue
in the dark
she sees the crooked smile
of the night sky
speckled freckles glitter
if only it were tender
instead
it's a torrent of inner resentment
she tried the bang
but the whimper pushed
from her lungs
before she could swallow it
captured in the mouths
of a trillion tiny awakenings

Wrapping arms around herself
she's unconsciously seeking her edges
so she can erase them
meld into the nebulous
liquid
sometimes
she imagines herself multiplied
stacked horizontal
her bodies
piled up
high as factory smoke stacks
vapouring messages
into the sky

who will guard
the azure once the clouds
have dissipated

deep breath

She knows the rare
moments of tranquillity
are not really hers
she doesn't own them
they're borrowed
loaned by the wind
or moon
or the voices of leaves
speaking riddled chants into the vacuum
swallowed
        suffocated

Her hands are often
around her throat
silence is a new pursuit
stillness a three piece suit
her two restless legs
refuse to wear
sleep
circumvents her exhaustion
until she's dreaming of slumber
wide eyed
wild eyed

while she paces
beneath that crooked smile
envious of all those secrets
released for relief
hers are still held close
in the fists she makes
when her fingers are free
of her neck

The speckled freckled sky
knows what's up
it's watching this unravelling
having witnessed millions
fall apart
she's not special
there's nothing extraordinary
about her suffering
nothing remarkable about her pain

Except that it's hers
she holds it close
like a new born
cradling the fragile head
in case it snaps back
frees itself from the neck

Don't we all hold our misery
like it were fragile
she wonders

pacing
beneath that crooked smile
she wonders
what's so funny
to the dark
she wonders
until each wondering
is shattered glass
she asks her ancestors to step in
whispers a little prayer to them

No one's coming to rescue you
she thinks to herself
sits
blinks
once twice
three times
then finally
when the crooked smile is fading
into dawn's radiant embrace
rests her head to sleep

Before it disappears completely
because the speckled freckled sky
knows what's up
it takes her secrets
out of her still clenched fists
and releases them up high

...

revoke

the horizon
a flat lining heartbeat
encroaching darkness
retracting all
until the formlessness
stays the madness
       fluttering breath
       the wings of bats overhead

remember when you
used to envy her pillow
permitted to retain
her sweat scent spit

the sky
is a liar
tall tales still
in thin moving clouds
the threatened downpour dissipating
the promised cleanse diminishing

remember when every
dip and curve was
your revered nation
religion and patriotism
suddenly consummate in
your previously anarchic being
as your fingers
whispered secrets down her belly

the trees
are sentinels
protecting the no ones
protecting them

in the shade
she's most brilliant
parts of her hidden

remember when excuses
tumbled from between lips
still wet from her lips
still wet from your cunt

the sun
made from bees
vibrates mightily
burning even the most
conscientious as though to
prove a point

remember when she
started disappearing into
her ugliness
flushed cheeks fresh
with 'fuck you'-s so violent
your breath left
erratic patterns in your chest
connect the dots gone all wrong

the birds
a cacophony
of ordered chaos
a crowd of witnesses
crowing at dawning rituals

remember when tea
scalded both
your tongues
each morning
but even that
couldn't burn the
laughter out of you
both

the earth
unsteady shifting
not half as strong
as its reputation
a mass of impermanence

remember when she
realised you could die
denied it every day
until she fled
across that lying sky
into that beatless
horizon

..?

the wanting

my wanting
is not so simple
not as you imagine it to be

intricate as knotted
gnarled tree roots
beneath a surface

my wanting
is made up of
fragments pieces loosely

s
   ca
                 t
         t
     e
         r
       ed

across regions
innerscapes
that once mattered

it is your job to
quell this hunger
gather me

collect then connect
all the parts
seek those missing

entice me with an
understanding that surprises me
surpasses my own

know me so completely
I need not know myself
anything anymore

the knowing tires me
exhausts me so
my mind barelyrestsrescueme

from sinking white pages
I attempt to devour with ink
blank unfathomable whiteness

I can't stand empty pages
I must overwhelm them
disarm them

moments
conjured to relieve me
scorched into my very being

I am branded
by these moments
I must monopolise this space

with sounds
forming words
to squander to your ears

hear me
loud and clear
allow me to become deaf to my own

wanting
save me from that silence
        whenitbecomestoomuch

I don't believe anybody
likes solitary moments
how can anyone like loneliness

a confinement made of memories
Balls and chains of recollections
partly manufactured anyway

through retelling
retelling
and photos

my wanting
plays tricks with the eyes
should I glance only at you

here I'm looking swallowing
devouring you whole pupils wide
so you can barely see the whites

do not get
tangledupinmygaze
endeavouring to trap you

into loving me
do not mistake that look
as burning for you

I am wet instead
with question marks
it's those I drown in

so their curves
wrap around me
their dots poke and prod

until I am awhirl with so much
confused wanting
I am sinking

you must preserve the will within me
stem the loss of words
from out the corners of my mouth

with kisses which fill
whatever may be empty
do not

underestimate this wanting
which never wavers
only worsens

what will be wasted if I cease
not the wanting

      notthewanting

...

Draw Breath

Thump of feet on concrete
breath in belly not chest
outrunning the beast
that beckons it bellows
above the sound of the ocean
that bawls the waves are braying

at the shore

She's praying to move past
the sweat that stings eyeballs
to fly up the stairs that deny her air
she's propelled by hindsight
winded by desire
spurred by a loneliness that

the slope of success doesn't soften

She's often lost in the wishes
of others as if she could be
what they can't It's a heavy burden
to be buried so she hides it in her blood
those cells are bled out from veins

too thick to know they've been cut

Who will carry her now she is a dead
weight prostrate under the load of knowing
there are those who perceive intimacy

from the words she's forming
true communion is a fallacy
when the discourse falls apart

Gentle power desire flesh
the words that beckon
these ebb the back flow
a tug a current that draws
them deeper under the influence
of what if maybe

this is where the abstract lives

Between the lines drawn
        breath exhale
it all needs to be spoken
the nuanced is lost on her
in these moments she has only words
but cannot speak poetry

she cannot draw breath

in a chest constricted by
unspoken prose
she is an unfinished sentence
kneeling before the grave
of an unknown
weeping for a lost love

she understands

the ridiculousness the drama
between each sob is hysterical laughter
others jog on through this graveyard

the immense yearning to be
closer to the earth
she can't help but think that everybody
is ultimately boxed up boxed in

Ocean roar wave wave
your froth and sea spray
strain at the limits of your own
rhythmic persistence
as the spittle drips from lips nostrils
flared nose running
the sleeve is a cumbersome tissue
it can't be scrunched up
tossed into the water to be soaked
float for a moment
translucent lost in the whitewash

until she is nothing more than
a bubble in your immensity

What existence is this slow suicide
each day closer to dying
sped up somewhat by the smoke she's inhaling

blowing rings round herself
forcing her feet to jump through
those hoops

She has known all about sex-hatred-anger-
love-greed-need-belief-denial-desire-
demands-failings-politics-war
-vulnerability-truth-lies-humanity
she has never known herself

they have never learned her off by heart

then loved her still
never memorised her heartbeat
as she did theirs
never copied her rhythm
forgiven her for the crime
of loving too hard
too much of the time

always mistook her compassion for weakness

wiped their feet on her mercy
til she was dirty hurting
she can't tell them this is how
one inseminates hate

.

She is still dried eyes baited breath
emptiness a gulf in her belly
standing feet uneven
on a rocky outcrop
the ocean gestures beckons
against boulders slaps and sprays

arms crossed eyes staring daring the ocean up

willing the foam to stretch skyward
to transform into a lover's arm
draw her down into the thrash boom
demanding they switch places
so it knows her world she its

this is the stand off

...

exposed

I wonder what you look like
under your skin

are they evident
the dreams I've etched in

sketched are lines
angles to begin

this feeling of want
with its pinprick sting

I've watched your body move
underneath mine

I wanted to see
if your heart beat in time

let me place a hand
over that spot

listen as you whisper
for me not to stop

sweat glistens in light
not meant to shine

it means your eyes
easily meet mine

ours is a rhythm
that can't be denied

I'll connect every spot
on your body

play them
like musical notes

let me pretend
it's a score I wrote

can they connect
me to you

if I mark them in black ink
beneath the surface

make them
a tattoo

the world could waste away
here I will stay

trapped in these moments
where I feast on us

enjoy the ascent to this
self-imposed banishment

a nation of pleasures
divine and our right

I'll keep my eyes tightly closed
while you stroke my hair

This experience
has left me bare

...

the eventuality of the path they walk

And then there were two
        one prone to drama the other to deflect
        both filled with love and a slow oozing regret

The threat of the ending looms larger
        as they clasp words around each other
        building bars out of exclamation
        meting out hurtful sentences
        barking accusations of righteousness
        bare teeth seethe about what they each perceive
        to be the ultimate wrong doing

They are fending off
        the incoming tsunami of wasted emotions
        no one wants to be left alone
        in an ocean of surplus devotion
        they take turns watching each other flounder
        as long as it protects them from ingesting
        a gut-full of salt water tears shed on an unmade bed
        so rumpled it's hard to rest their weary heads
        to recover from previously wandering eyes
        pondering on moments untold not unnoticed

They begin to
        smother one another under a quilt of guilt
        somewhere within the grim din of their clanking hearts
        they realise the reserves they are banking on
        are running dangerously low on returns

Once the seed of doubt has been planted
      great big branches of uncertainty spread their limbs
      over harbours of suspicion
      no longer are questions asked
      instead accusations are made
      these lovers gnaw at each other
      until they reach the bone
      both know the eventuality of the path they walk
      yet inertia propels them forwards
      towards destination frustration

They oscillate between
      treading on eggshells
      all out emotional wars
      doors are slammed
      upon which potential attacks bounce off
      not before they've made some indelible mark
      like that of Cain their pain stains them
      more than that their pain maims them
      so that violent strides become mere limps
      they stop moving forwards seem to shift backwards
      in a slow motion drowning of their unrelenting desires
      whilst simultaneously being fuelled
      by the wrong kind of fires

Neither of them knows how long they can sustain it
      both know they will remain in it
      until the last verbal punch is laid squarely
      between the eyes of confrontation

until they're both winded
from over-analytical conversation
hate-filled debates and coarse curses
until their embraces become less placatory more exploratory
their kisses impassioned again their desires
reminding them of the complete beat of two
so that suddenly the raft
which dragged them out into a sea of rough emotions
is now a smooth sailing yacht upon calm waters
hindsight makes an example of them
experiences help to build the foundation
they believe in each other enough to know

though one is prone to drama the other to deflect
it's what keeps them strong and in check
and then there were two

...

Our hearts

Our hearts only beat once
     the second is an echo
     in a chamber of emptiness
     our chests leave room for breath
     but still welcome death
     come the day we can no longer inhale

     sitting on the wind
     besides pollen and insects
     are tiny symphonies
     we have forgotten to listen for
     we have lost our voices
     forgotten to sing
     beauty beats a mute rhythm
     whilst ugly drums louder

Our hearts once unlocked
     to a universe connected to us
     have become blackened by the soot
     and dust of constant violence
     we seek to protect ourselves from the barrage
     of blasphemies and brutal behaviour
     against what once made us human
     we have switched off
     we exhale little combination codes
     that no one could ever know

     now the wind is laden
     with the letters N and O

Our hearts are no longer red
        instead sit black and blue
        bruised and broken
        from all things left unspoken
        those colours spread
        through the rest of us
        so we speak angry words

        having forgotten the language of forgiveness
        we sit and witness the barren landscape of time
        passing the infinite has become finite
        as a night filled with wind whispering
        forget me not though the sun will rise
        it dawns on a place with no space for love

Our hearts no longer have strings
        to be plucked they have been silenced
        behind walls great fortresses
        we are no longer
        kings and queens of our castles
        we are slaves to a state of being

we should never have embraced

...

stick to the left wall and run

the sun sets slowly at first pinks oranges reds blues vying for your
gratitude soft clouds float catching light low smoke from cigarettes
being blown by mouths forming O's into half empty wine glasses
of Shiraz which your palm covers to trap some sense of visible
breath you need to see it in the physical form otherwise you're
gasping grasping onto something that isn't really yours grappling
with that constant heightened state both familiar and forlorn you're
convincing yourself there are no immediate threats here just idle
regrets that come in on the mist to make themselves known they'll
stay just long enough to make sure what matters is swept away so
guilt can settle in call you home dissipate dissolve into the night
which is coming forget those regrets were ever present at all // a
sliver of a moon rises flanked by stars that outshine it the shadows
bring noises reflecting the mood of your heart smells are caught
on the breeze brought to your nose a universal offering they've
swept through the paddock of those memories you're still traipsing
through less paddock more maze you remember someone once
told you if you end up in a labyrinth stick to the left wall and run
until blood is pumping coursing through veins reminding you life
is in the physical existence slips through your fingertips when you
focus on the semantics too much don't think too much run until
your feet ache sweat pours down your face you are not porcelain
you will not break not if you run stick to the left wall run // the
sun rises with little fanfare the clouds gathered force during the
night decided it was their turn to take over the sky light shimmers
with a feeble attempt to shine the wine is finished your glass stands
empty begging to be refilled your mind hasn't stopped hasn't even
slowed you've spent your night running you are beyond tired your
eyes have taken over from the night as the shadows' employer

you're seeking poetry in the places you've been this evening so
sanity may be fooled into thinking the journey was intentional
you are seeking the saviour that will let you in to sleep suddenly
your fingers are awake taking messages from the spirits hoping
something will be cleansed from this feeling overcome with the
desire to describe delegate letters so they group in sentence that
begin with I end with you anything to prove to yourself you have
reason through rhyme you have bought yourself more time but
nothing has been filled there is no concrete on those pages only
thoughts ephemeral a beating heart never appeases it's hard to be
still when that sense of ill makes you feel you'll never be full that
hole that you've spent most your life trying to fill remains gaping
your want growing even now still shrill

...

Ancestral Homage

I am my grandfather's memories
of sunshine streaming through olive trees
women sitting clucking like hens
as they crush garlic with spices
to make that night's meal
the men tend gardens plough fields
of their 'baladi' their homeland

I am my grandfather's memories
remembering he was raised a Christian
in a land of Muslims with Jewish friends
he played in the dirt with future enemies
shared meals didn't yet know history
was in the making somewhere in Europe

I am my grandfather's memories
the things he doesn't even know yet
one of millions of pawns negotiated
in a deal to alleviate the guilt of the world
for crimes committed he had no hand in
there was no hatred yet

I am my grandfather's nightmares
stories became horrors
that caressed his ears his parents'
others in their community whispering
about death wiping out whole villages
mass graves being filled blood being shed
so much that rivers ran along their earth

turning it crimson
violence was making the 'arrad' arid land
once fertile wasted

I am my grandfather's nightmares
where he wished to be deaf
to the stories of the 'nakba'
where to stay was to die
where to leave was to die
death comes in many forms
when your feet no can longer touch
the dirt you took your first steps on
it becomes a form of death too

I am my grandfather's memories
of the stories coming closer
terror being sowed whilst peasants
ploughed the land he thought of the danger
his ageing parents were in
thought of his own life ahead of him
seen his people torn from the earth
no more roots they wandered out
dazed confused crying for their losses
mourning the dead asking 'allah'
what they did to deserve this
he'd seen whole villages razed to the ground
he knew a knock on the door imminent
the violence ravaging his land intensified daily
knowing under occupation is no place to live

he left saying goodbye to his parents
he swore he would send for them
once he had found somewhere safe

I am my grandfather's memories
as he stepped out the door one last time
held his hand up to shield his eyes
breathed in slow through his nostrils
forced himself to remember every smell
opened his eyes wide allowed them to sting
looked upon his village one last time
forced himself to remember every sight
closed his eyes committed to memory
all those memories before 1948
so he would leave in love not hate
opening his eyes
I am his memory of walking away
of the crunch of dirt beneath his feet
listening to the earth's conversation with him
the wind wishing him well through trees
he talked back with his heart
knowing he wouldn't return
he swore to his homeland
it would reside forever inside

I am my grandfather's memories
as he emigrated to Lebanon
to try to start again working long hours
as a refugee in a foreign land

trying to gather money required
to save his parents from a death beckoning

I am my grandfather's memories
as he managed to bring his parents over
then start his own family
getting married having children
tragically losing a wife getting married again
having more children
trying to provide for them

I am my father's memories
of being born into a displaced family
where the homeland is referred to constantly
the sense he belonged elsewhere
injustice keenly felt but where the world
seemed not to care nor understand
the plight of his people

I am my father's memories
of a family striving to survive
always on the outside he a child
growing in another war-torn country
knowing he would leave
before the army could get to him

I am my father's memories
of being kidnapped twice
twice being set free

as he did not subscribe to
any form of religious extremism

I am my father's memories
of constant warfare being shot
by rubber bullets choking on tear gas
listening to missiles soar overhead
hoping against all hope
their bullet-riddled apartment block
would not be hit next

I am my father's memories
of being 18 and knowing if he did not leave
he would have to bear a weapon
so he left that land
knowing that he could never return
he became a deserter of a war
he did not agree with
as the plane ascended towards the heavens
I am his memories of hope
for a better future
sadness he may never see those he loves again

I am my father's memories
of picking grapes in France
trying to save enough money to get further
away

I am my father's memory
of boarding a plane for Australia
where he knew my mother to be
tearing up his passport
arriving as a refugee

I am my own memory
of being eight or nine years old
listening to the voice of my grandfather
on a tape he's sent us from a land
I can barely imagine
but whose music I hear whose food I eat
whose history I am already learning

I am my own memory
of being 10 or 11 years old
seeing my Dad cry for the first time
my father knew his father was dying
and couldn't return
he didn't get to say goodbye
to his 'Baba' on his deathbed
that's when I became
my grandfather's memories
he could no longer remember
now that he had been buried

I am my own memory
of being a teenager struggling to exist
between two cultures

one which demanded I hang onto a past
one which forced me into the future
one which filled me with love
one which forced me to belong to this land

I am my own memory
of trying to understand
why my father was always so angry
until I was old enough to see
where once my father had been a warrior
he was now nothing more than a worrier
I mistook that fear at losing his family his land –
everything I took for granted – for anger

I am my family's blood
where these memories histories
course through my veins
where my own feet have not yet touched
the soil of where my great grandfather
my grandfather and my father's
footsteps roamed

I am the memories
of the displaced lost hidden
lies propaganda hatred

I am the memories
of blue skies dry heat homous
tabouli tabla

I am the memories
of that lost land
and another occupied land
gained

...

Break Me

End me
                    fuck all the others
                        out of me
                      breath by breath
              so you are all I inhale
              only then can I forget
          there's an entire world
                      banging against
                        my ribcage
                    drive those lovers
                  beyond the reaches
              of my recollections
                  devour longings
                    originally born
                  from distant flesh
                            my
                      own displayed
                            so
                      that you may

Bruise me

let it all rush to the
surface sitting
beneath
transparent skin
ready to crack
creating crevices
like when things
first shifted
tore apart split
so you
have no choice
but to

Spill me

there must be
blood tears
which travel terrain
your hands and lips
have already covered
your body smothering
so what is known
is a trinity
of godlessness
spread me
vulnerable

over what we'll never be
stretched sweat-
drenched slick
with a desperate
sickness to be ruined
this illness
gives me strength
so you can

Degrade me

let humiliation be
the confrontation
between what's
primal ego
created inherent
the division
of what is animal human
reduce me to a mess
so complete I'm a mass
of trembling limbs
shuddering torso
taut mouth
ringing ears
dizzy enough
for you to

Finish me

you have my permission
this is a consensual ending
of the conscious self
I wish to see
my own mortality
behind lids clenched
blinded to all else
I will create the visions
required for rebirth
reborn from the detritus
of basic elements
you me fucking until

I am wasted

collapsed
in upon myself forced to rebuild
cell by cell
my lips stained
with your name
every breath
released a calling
an intonation of
wanting a chant
reflected
in multiple mirrors

so that its echo
is limitless
and while rebounding
off the walls of my need
to be annihilated
I will breathe
long enough for you
to become
the rouge in my cheeks
the blood that gathers
to spell what I can't say
the drops of sweat
that sit between
shoulder blades
I will become
that sigh not held
that cry unrestrained
so I am broken
only then will I open up
again

...

inner/e/scape

She watches shadows meander close...thinking about how reality can be a fluid thing...no one warned her about that...moving in and out of focus...blurred lines...fluent languages of self-loathing...anxiety...how to silence the inner monologue which talks the self into torment... torturing instead of speaking tolerance...living with one hand in her pocket...the other on her heart...she's learnt the art of filling the air with other people's lungs...so that when it wells...she can still draw breath...the lines of the horizon stretch dive dip...almost near enough to touch...with eyes closed...never near enough to reach...

The shadows stray at the edges of light... they're carrying night in packs...she's not ready to welcome in the darkness...for it to spill unconfined...for stars to stain her sky... she's thinking about words...how they crawl spidery out of some mouths to weave webs she's easily caught in...how other times they tumble uninterrupted...a torrent of tragic truths...to change everything...unable to be shoved back in...she's a deluge of diamonds on ice...a cacophony of agony...yelling back the horizon...warning it not to come near...

The shadows drift closer...she's been seeking something in the eyes of others brown blue even green...searching for some sense of a collective humanity...wondering if there's any unhindered intimacy left...she tries to hold their gaze with a need to create heat burning in her...she knows time has no temperature... when she tells them this their eyes fill with tiny glaciers...no matter how hot she gets she has a hard time melting ice bergs...she moves from face to face to face to face to face...someone should tell her...you can't see the horizon...in people's pupils...

The shadows snake slowly trying a different tack to take over...wondering if she'll notice... she's busy thinking about how she asked them to wait...where the wind pauses where wings are a musical movement instead...where the grass is a bed to rest all weary heads...she's always been a lucid dreamer lost in musings... which makes it hard to live in the real world... harsh and heavy brash and fleshy...if she creates a really good fantasy...one colourful... laden with all that's lovely...maybe she can lure the horizon in...

The shadows are getting rowdy...never mind she's lost in a reverie...wondering about her need to be near water at all times...the waves are sirens...grains of sand slaves to the wind...when she can't float she calls for her ship...a captain even when sinking...when truth pitches it side to side...and she's battling seasickness...she knows the best remedy is to watch the horizon...but there's no way to focus when you're sick and sinking...

The shadows won't take no for an answer... she's thinking about death...having lived half her life on knees bent...shoulders hunched... she's decided she wants to be buried standing... the last meal of a worm...soon to be airborne... digested in the belly of a bird...that horizon... closer than it's ever been...she can almost feel its defining line...a finality...take her there... soar beaked beauty...allow her the type of freedom she only ever sees in movies

...

arrhythmic nocturne

These things we have impressed
on each other through flesh
will be left in bed between sheets
expressed through the feeling
of skin on skin locked eyes wavering

trying not to seem too connected
pretending there is such a thing
as momentary new beginnings
my heart lies to my head
pretends I do detached sex well

that every stranger
I've shed layers with
remained a stranger to me
I have collected parts of every lover
not as notches nor skinned scalps

but small secrets in a vault that keeps us
connected though years have passed
there have been lasting marks
that I recall when times
travel through the light and dark

this heart is a sucker
for intense connection
these things we have impressed
upon each other as strangers
who momentarily love

cannot be jotted down on paper
which only knows the existence of
white black I cannot type
the name of every sense
expecting it to do the act justice

like the feel of goosebumps
on raised hips under fingertips
that declare their individuality
though fingerprints and specific wantings
are often linked and haunt me

like the sensation of breath on neck
before teeth sink in
biting flesh begging to be marked
for short lived ownership
denying the politically correct

momentarily we are both sacrificed
at the altar of what is wrong
these forbidden things cannot be
dealt through hands of cards
stacked precariously

a house that will come tumbling
on what cannot be said
because legs have been spread
on beds where begging for sex
is part of a splayed sensuality

before spirits
have even had a chance
to couple
I'm not one to say no to desire

the emptiness after
is simply a craving
for each lover to know me better
for more than a night
filled with split seconds

begging to be reckoned with
beckoning sensations
to remind us that every bit of society
that deadens us can be ripped apart
by slippery allies such as we

who pretend
that when bodies collide
it is to satisfy
some primal instinct
some physical genetic imprint

but I believe it is more to do with
the early loss of innocence
sought to be reborn
from constant diffidence
we become two dissidents

from society's pressures
to be normal
through touch we can undo
any pretence
of constant self-control

keeping ourselves in check
until we can be released
through those rhythms nocturnal
still I seek these things
that petite mort

from hands that will not know me more
whose caresses I will allow
to undress only small parts of me
as much as I crave
some deeper knowledge and knowing

I understand that once flesh
has been redressed
hair straightened tied back
lamps turned off
lights switched on

a hurried kiss at a closing door
what most of us are running from
we cannot be mirrors
for strangers without clearer vision
and welcoming danger

allowing them nearer
enclosed chambers
and whispering to them
how naming such things
will change us

...

Guatemalan waters

Remember
          truth resides
          just behind the eyes
lies aren't so easy to see
when they're told by one
you're willing to believe

she said

hennaed hands fluttering
towards her hair
bare shoulders dark as mochas
I hadn't sipped in eternities

They sent me to a priest
after I told them god didn't exist
he offered me a vaginal massage
to help bring god close again

her laughter glitters in the sun's rays
like the pollen which tickles my nostrils
bells on her ankles tinkle
as we walk through cement parks

where men in army fatigues
clutch weapons at the ready
in case bird shit covered statues
try to make a run for it

I love to dance
take my chances with
middle eastern rhythms
especially on a full moon

I feel something frantic forming
calling my name
being in a full room
all eyes on me
I like to believe I'm mesmerising

he doesn't like it
calls me a slut
as though being born
with this cunt
were my fault

pushing him like I do
is like pouring salt
in the wound

a self-deprecating smile
plays on her lips
tears gather but hold

I turn to the river
racing as it has been from
Guatemala

escaping heavy rain
drowning rocks in its rush to
get out get away get gone

...

don't look down

       your scars
a brutal beautiful
forging through life
even as death's gristly hold
tries to drag you down
the jagged edges of scar tissue
something like a zipper
you joke
       will be your next tattoo

       dust particles
tap dance off furniture edges
light splayed like the sun's
split wide trying to say
'look at my hot stuff babe'
while the pain rides
       every internal nerve

       you are wound tight
like when you were young
you'd wrap rubber bands
round your pinkie
blood gathering at the tip
til it turned purple
suddenly you'd be afraid
the swelling making it
harder to remove the elastic
your panic a pin prick spreading
       swiftly

that sensation is
your every day
the opiates a liquid dip
muting a little more
with every hit
your fingers trace
again those battle lines
on flesh carved
     with tiny knives

     people dip their heads
over the precipice
just to feel their breath
catch in their chests
you would give anything
to be able to scrabble back
     from the ledge

...

dance it all away

sitting on the roof top
bass thumping
club reverberating
ecstasy thick in blood stream
all around me
people gladly drowning in k-holes
this is what it is to exist
in the midst of a tightening fist
like giants we stalked halls
made for the lingering
whilst animals pelted us with eggs
off pedestrian bridges
I did not mind wiping the yolk
off my face
I was not afraid of their hate
just pitied their small lives
and minds
where I sat surrounded
by love rainbows and glitter
they were lost in bitter histories
as the future thrust forward
without them
and we were the dreamers
who knew the inevitable would
eventuate eventually –
we just didn't know
it would take this long
and how long it takes
while we shake our arses

to encrypted music
tunes laced with longing
you can only hear
if you've lived it
the others are thrashing
to instrumental damage
and my heart is aching
like my dance-weary feet
because the drugs are ebbing
and once again
I'm driving home semi-high
the freeway a road to captivity
the wind whipping my hair
my jaw grinding
fingers tapping the steering wheel
as a symphony of electrodes
plays out of distorting car speakers
we were momentary gods flung
into a stratosphere
strung up by our own irreverence
untouchable until now
back here on earth
the asphalt rises up to meet me
white lines a new age cage
their rage a pitter patter
across wide pupils
leaving an indelible mark
on this bluff heart

...

Pregnant

(for feature film SLAM)

Mother they will not make me forget
they cannot silence this tongue
these stories
from your womb to my mouth

your fears and your strength
I carry your cells
in my particles
your atoms
in my blood
I am made of you
your displacement
men gather
stripping people
of the earth beneath their feet
not caring dirt is sacred
dirt beneath nails
magic from which
olive trees flourish
produce fruit
produce oil
thick and golden
like light
pouring across
invaders as they
push back the line

Men and their ability
to make the innocent guilty
as though we perpetuate
our own genocide
mother
they push back the line
with bulldozers rifles
missiles white phosphorus
massacres and mass graves
imprisoning the young
so they will never grow
into warriors
stones from their hands
transferred to stones in their shoes
so they sink quick
in the sorrows
of those who mourn them

Mother they will not make me forget
they cannot silence this tongue
these stories
from your womb to my mouth

Like here in this nation
birthed by genocide
stripping people
of the red earth beneath their feet
not caring that red earth
is sacred

magic from which
dreaming flourished
producing songlines
like music pouring
into ears deaf to it
only hearing their own
righteousness
but I'm not deaf
I am trying to learn
the language of dreamtime
so I can teach you mother
there are stories of survival
buried deep
in this red earth
she speaks in fervent whispers
I am listening

Mother they will not make me forget
they cannot silence this tongue
these stories
from your womb to my mouth

About how we were poets
long before they knew
the glory of poetry
how we were sculptors
philosophers
long before they
branded us terrorists and savages

backwards and undemocratic
they cannot understand
sometimes the hijab is a choice
as woman empowered
outside the male gaze
because they will not
read her by her curves
but by the fierceness
of her words

these stories
are our lifeblood
we are impregnated with history
and the resilience
of our women warriors
instruments of strength
against the devastating
actions of men
who have never cared
for consequence

but they will not make me forget
they cannot silence this tongue
these stories
from your womb to my mouth

we know the strength
in sharing truth
lips to ears

hearts to souls
this is how we rise up
gather strength
become a force to be reckoned with
refuse to submit
to assimilate
their continued colonisation
will not abate
so we must
destroy those who would
dictate the ways we should live
the dirt from beneath our fingernails
shows we are no strangers
to hard work –
dismantling the system
bolt by bolt
crushing white supremacy
fist to fist
the only language
the white tongue understands is
violence
violence must be met with
violence
we shall not remain silent

We are stomping untruths
into that white abyss
let them hear truth echoed back
as we bleed these stories

etched into our existence
we are going to show them
mother
no matter how hard they try
to silence us
they will never fully understand
the power inside
our resilience that ensures
we will always survive

...

Afterword

Anna Kerdijk Nicholson

I first met Candy Royalle, to talk to, at the Awards Ceremony for the Marten Bequest Travelling Scholarship in 2012.

Previously, I'd seen her on stage at the Australian Poetry Festival in Kings Cross. She told me a long time later that it was an important invitation, where she felt recognised by the mainstream, endorsed by the 'page poetry' establishment. Which was what Brook Emery and Martin Langford did – they were catholic in their tastes, broadly read and wonderful curators. I was in the audience close to the front. I think Anya Walwicz performed in that set. Candy had dreadlocks and charisma. Chris Wallace-Crabbe was the keynote. They are all such wonderful, different poets. Candy didn't seem to have the luxury of being humorous or aloof from her subject matter, she was an activist and her words were wet with calls to action or the fluids of love-making.

Back to the Marten Bequest awards: I was one of three judges of the poetry award and I just happened to be the one who made the announcement and gave the speech. There were some fervent and powerful applications that round – only one would be awarded. Candy wasn't the one. She came up to me after the announcement and introduced herself and her girlfriend, Nic. She brushed off some tears. 'It doesn't matter that I didn't get the grant, I'll crowdfund myself to do the project anyway,' she said, and beamed that million-megawatt Candy smile. She was going to two schools of performance poetry, one in England, the other in Scotland, and giving performances along the way. She already had venues and bookings. The woman was a powerhouse, more in the mould of an emerging rock star than my experience of an emerging poet.

The three of us bumped into each other again as I was putting on my bike helmet for my ride home. After some chatting about pushbikes, Candy said to me 'I want you to be my mentor'. I said 'That's all well and good but we come from very different genres of poetry. I will not take you on as a mentee unless I can contribute to your career – I don't have contacts inside performance poetry, I'm not sure I've got an idea of what excellence in the form entails. My role as a mentor is to give you entrees to people and opportunities, to understand your goals and help you fulfil them.'

Not daunted, never daunted – that's what you read in the eulogies after her death, about her courage and her activism, her big loving heart – Candy said 'but will you meet with me, even if it's just once?' I said 'Yes, let's meet for an hour and you can interview me and I'll interview you – we have to form a team which is willing to make plans and work together to get them done. If either of us thinks it won't work, then we can go our separate ways.'

And meet we did. Our first meeting was at a café in Surry Hills which had a library-like area upstairs and we sat in leather bucket seats across a table and we probed into one another's willingness to work, explained our differences and heard, I think, things which delighted us both. Candy got a poet-mentor, but a professional lawyer who ran her own CBD business with years of professional mentoring under her belt, with decades of involvement in poetry and its organisation, structures and a knowledge of its organs, opportunities, grant-applications and acquittals and the flux of magazines, editors and publishers. I got a poet-mentee, but a superb administrator and organiser with unlimited energy, conviction and talent paired with negotiating skills, charisma and goal-setting.

I used the phrase 'goal-setting' carefully because I could have used, as she did self-deprecatingly to me, 'ambition'. Laughing, she said 'I have enough ambition and ego for us both': disarming, charming but, in context, this self-deprecating comment was in response to a negotiation about editing. Candy wanted me to work with her to produce a 'page-poem' from a performance piece. 'I can tell you the unstated rules or I can edit the work and you'll see from the ink how the forms differ,' I offered. Any poet, I think, crafts their work and cleaves to it. Subjectivity, especially in a lyrical or visceral poetry like Candy was writing – means the subject and form are one with the creator; and the creator is likely to be cut by unsubtle criticism or suggestions for change. So it could have been with Candy, but she had, she said, 'enough ambition and ego for both of us' and she was willing to allow me loose on this piece of work she had made – and had performed many times to an adoring public.

When we looked at the suggestions together, her reaction was intellectual. It was one of the great pleasures of working with her that she always gave so much, and came from a deep and wise place. She was amazed at the conventions of page poetry: 'but audiences go wild when I perform this piece, why cut the repetition, why remove the antiquated modes of speech, why change the lineation?' It was a valid challenge: why these conventions, how do I know what I know, what allows me to be an editor, a suggester, an attempted improver of others' work?

Candy challenged me (and challenges me still) to put these things into words. To sit on the other side of the poetry table from her and view 'page poetry' objectively: to give its CV, its credentials, the rationale for my possibly effete, nepotistic, under-stated, self-indulgent, politically light-on (if not apolitical) art form, probably comprised of what Candy saw as a wall of complacent white straight folk. A great mentor/mentee relationship, I now know, fosters growth in both people.

When we started meeting, there was no cancer diagnosis. We met at Yulli's in Surry Hills. I rode my pushbike there, she her motorbike. After our regular monthly intense hour, we'd end up putting on our helmets, she unleashing the yard of dreadlocks from their tether so she could get her crash-lid over them. They hung down to the top of her legs. I bunged my cycle helmet over my short business crop. She'd be talking about life now, that she needed to move out of Tamarama, the end of a relationship, the spark of a journey. The work − her soul-baring, sexy work − was doing its job, bringing us together as friends. Twenty years between us, but respectful, caring, interested. You will find much of her life in this book. You will be able to smell and taste it. You will feel the power of her and her courage.

Then came the first hospitalisation and the cancer diagnosis. She proudly showed me the great long abdominal scar and got back to work. Not just on her own pieces, but she worked for the good of others. She brought together a bunch of her poetry contemporaries to workshop their pieces and support each other on their paths. She started hosting Word in Hand poetry community gigs at the Friend in Hand and then at the Red Rattler, supporting her fellow poets and her art form. She was a professional poet: she lived on the earnings from her art. At first she had part-time work in the city, but eventually she was earning enough from commissions, prizes, teaching, giving workshops, hosting the Walkleys, performances and album- and book-sales to resign from her city job.

She put tickets at the door for me twice. The first time at the Red Rattler in Marrickville where she was playing with Sloppy Joe. It was a rock concert. She was mesmerising. Such talent she worked along-side – burlesque performers, musicians. There I got to meet her parents and I'm very glad. Her petite and feminine mum, her large, quiet dad, their pride in their outrageous, queer, talented daughter. She played that gig in an outfit she made herself, her legs bound in ribbons of black cloth and bare feet. Those soft-soled feet stamped the stage, beating out the rhythm of the verse – she sang her poems, she narrated the journey of the show, this was a professional theatrical performance celebrating all the other artists on stage with her, not a one-woman show.

The second time she put tickets at the door for my friend, Annie, who was also living with cancer. This time it was for *The Lady & the Unicorn* 2018 exhibition at the Art Gallery of NSW, where she was the third of 3 performers. I hugged her so hard after the show, I banged my cheekbone into hers – now prominent, she now thin. 'Was it OK, I felt I couldn't give it my all?' So uncharacteristic. I thanked her for getting Annie's ticket and introduced them. She said 'Tell Annie she has strength. Tell her not to think about the time that's left at all, tell her to think about the things she wants to get done'. It was how she was managing her own journey with cancer. She never once spoke about her prognosis, only about what she needed to do.

For that first hour's meeting, back in 2012, I asked her to put together a personal statement, like an avowal, from the present through to 20 years' time. 'In five years, I am …', she wrote; 'in ten years, I am …'. In 2018, she has already achieved so much of what she had described for herself.

Some months ago, I went to her flat in East Sydney and she made me mint tea in a pretty pot with its matching cup. She loved pottery. She had display cabinets to house her most cherished pieces. On the coffee table in front of us was a glamourous book entitled 'Butch'. 'This mint tea is the most delicious I've ever had.'

'It's my Mum's,' Candy said. 'She grows, dries and crumbles it herself.' I could see her Mum on the farm, in my mind's eye, and that tea tasted of the love between Candy and her Mum: you see the strength of that relationship and Candy's sense of inheritance in the last poem in the book. Candy showed me photos of her on the farm and where her place was on it, away from the home paddock. She padded around. We talked about the pain: where it was, how she managed it. There was much less of her now, but her skin and eyes were clear and she resembled her porcelainware, translucent but enormously strong. This was the woman who was writing about fucking, self-abasement, unrequited love, avatars of the Moon. She wanted, of all things, to have a book published by a reputable publisher. Unlike most poets, she had an agent. Her agent loved the first draft of her MS and on 6 April 2018 Candy's extraordinary good news was that her work had been accepted by UWA Publishing. 'I want you to be its editor and I want you to write a foreword.' 'I'd be honoured, but I'm not sure poetry presses permit a personal choice of editor…'. Not long afterwards, Candy confirmed that UWA Publishing had acceded to her requests. She was intending to write more poems for it during a writer-in-residency which she didn't get to attend.

And so it is that Candy has left the stage, and I'm sitting here on a stool, still hoping for her encore. It has been a rich and emotionally complex process, readying the manuscript for publication. I have not written here about Candy's technique or positioned the work within contemporary practice. I think it important that Candy speaks for herself.

When a writer dies before their book is published, they don't get to correct the proofs. The changes and the failings are mine. The talent and the trust are all Candy's.

ACKNOWLEDGEMENTS

To my dearest friends who have supported me in ways I never even dreamt possible: Nic, you are and will forever be my soulmate – thank you for still loving me; Nicole, I rediscovered my ancestors because of your inherent wisdom, you are magic; Emma Maye, you are my soul sister and being an alien goddess with you makes so much sense to me – you know they keep telling us no because they're so afraid we will, and babe, we are; Linda, your ever growing fierceness inspires me to be fearless; Stella, you nurture in ways undreamt; Tank, you have kept me so well fed, my freezer often full and every tiny morsel tastes like love; Niveen, let's make more music baby, let's dance to 90's RnB and hip hop until we drop; Felicity, you'll always be a 'quality street girl' to me.

To my amazing agent Jane Novak: you believed in me when the establishment didn't, said yes when I was so used to hearing no. Thank you for **seeing** me.

To my mentor and editor Anna Kerdijk Nicholson: look how far we've come! You will never know how much your belief in me as a late 20-something poet, pushed me forwards – you were the first one to open your door, thank you. And now, here we are!

NOTES

Some of the poems in this book have been published previously and some in a slightly different form. Acknowledgement and thanks to:

- The Austin International Poetry anthology 'Diver-city' which published *Impermanent* in 2012
- The World Poetry Cup 2012 for awarding *Ancestral Homage* first prize
- The Red Room Company which commissioned *That House* for publication in 2014
- The Queensland Poetry Festival which published *Let's call it art* in 2014 (originally titled *Ask*)
- Inkerman and Blunt which published *Entangled Part III* in 'Australian Love Poems' in 2014
- Overland Magazine, Audio Edition for publishing *Our hearts* (then titled *thrum hum*) in 2014
- Peril Magazine which commissioned *Vanquished* for publication in 2017
- The Red Room Company which commissioned *I tread this coastal path* (originally titled *Ebb no flow*) for publication in 2017.

Previously self-published work:

- The chapbook, 'Heartbeats', published 2012 which included:
  - *I will be a God without you* (originally titled *An Ode*)
  - *There is no poetry left in me today* (originally titled *Sonnet in skin*)
  - *Ancestral Homage* (originally titled *Memories*)
  - *Our Hearts*
- The chapbook, 'Love Spectacular', which included:
  - *the wanting* (originally titled *Escape*)
  - *exposed* (originally titled *Under your Skin*)
  - *the eventuality of the path they walk* (originally titled *and then there were two*)
- The album, 'Frida People', on which were recorded:
  - *Draw Breath*
  - *inner/e/scape* (originally titled *Shadows on the Horizon*)
  - *arrhythmic nocturne* (originally titled *They cannot be named*)
- The album, Stories by Starlight', on which was recorded *stick to the left wall and run* (originally titled *want still shrill*).